Coaching Questions:

How to Find Your Method to Become a Successful Coach

the owners themselves, not affiliated with this document.

Table of Contents

Introduction

Currently are not doubt about the impact of coaching in business, but to individuals too, and its scope extends to different areas of human development, in this context, its potential is immense; this in itself represents a very exciting outlook, the expectations of professionals dedicated to this activity are limited only it's only for its own capacity for innovation; It is their prerogative to be pioneers in times when everything seems to have been invented.

Are exposed multidisciplinary tools that allow the coach implement methodologies to project their own vision, talents, and skills in proposals of unique value for their coaches

Designed as a theoretical and practical system it allows to apply the concepts exposed to the personal and professional environment, providing the reader with a space to assimilate learning through their own experience along of the activities proposed in the text.

Fields of action: Criteria are proposed to establish the goals of progress considering the intellectual characteristics of the coach, his personal inclinations and career opportunities,

Based on measurable elements of evaluation, supported on marketing principles, psychology, and social dynamics.

Methodological design tools: Compendium of research systems, resources, creativity and action methodologies used in other disciplines, adapted to achieve objectives focused on coaching.

Readers will find the basics of Coaching, from its definition, its main branches, requirements for their performance, its benefits, the most common errors, as well as the lucrative aspects of this activity. It is an introductory guide that provides an overview of this new discipline, but of great relevance to today's society.

Charisma and communicational resources: Communication is the key tool of the coach, his success depends on how effectively he use it, and he should be aware of its systematic application, which becomes his personal distinctive. This book provides resources for articulating a method of communicational development.

They are constructed, over benchmarks of coaching international regulatory organizations, new skills that respond to the inertia of a society that evolves and requires management of human resources development in increasingly diverse and specialized facets. Opportunities will be there, for those who are attentive to take advantage of them.

Now, Welcome to the next phase of coaching.

Chapter 1 - Know the General Aspects of Coaching

What is coaching?

Because it is a multidisciplinary activity, the concept of Coaching has been misunderstood by those who do not know their fundamentals, and is often confused with mentoring, counseling, consulting, advisory and training, whose aims are similar, but their procedures are different.

Coaching is a process by which a client, or coaches, improve its effectiveness in some specific aspect of his personal life, or profession, through the intervention of a specialized professional who conducts a systematic dialogue, whose aim is that the coaches be aware of the actions that will lead him to achieve this improvement through some interview questions addressed him to think. From this premise a specific methodology that results in the different types of Coaching develops.

What situations can works a Coach?

Although fields, where a Coach can operate, are extensive, there are situations where the value of his participation is well identified:

Coaching is primarily focused on the development, a person who is well to be better but effectively treats people who require remedial situations.

• Success on goals life. When an individual feels the inner need to recover after a crisis or chronic stage of stagnation and despair and decides to fix it, but has lost sight of his own aspirations and him no longer conscience of how or why he does it.

• Breaking vicious circles. When an individual has not energy or hope to find by his own means the way to generate a new dynamic to increase his action potential, the aim focus is getting the client realizes what is unable or is unwilling to perceive at first instance. This relaxes the rigid and obsolete beliefs, and he transforms consciously his mindset to the evaluation of new ideas, new outcomes.

- There is confusion on distinguishing the priority objectives; The client does not know how to specify them;

- Like, kick start to encourage independence and initiative, optimizing own resources to achieve a purpose.

When is coaching effective?

In companies:

Coaching should apply when:

- Given a poor job performance, coaching works as a feedback tool to promote, from the personal conviction, actions excellence.

- To growth, the skills demonstrated by a promising key element in the company.

- To complement the skills a worker who needs to master in order to achieve optimal performance of their duties.

Effective coaching is characterized by positivism, confidence and rarely correction, which in turn is presented with the utmost restraint.

Why and how can the Coach help?

- The role of a Coach is to induce through dialogue a systematic and sincere reflection on the core of the conflict or goal, allowing to client exposing freely his thoughts and more legitimate concerns; the validity of beliefs code that he holds as an absolutely true is questioned to remove those that are incongruent with reality, to obtain an objective view of it, from which is set an action plan that the coaches must assume with conviction to set steps and deadlines for achieving them.

What are the benefits of being a coach?

- Being coach Means making a constant search and continues to personal and professional excellence;

- Develop the ability to interact in a conscious, fluid and secure with people of diverse temperaments;

- Helping others overcome their problems and through the experience of finding a way to self-knowledge and a fuller life;

- Achieve professional and financial freedom itself;

- Manage a career according to his own interests and areas of opportunity as a Coach

- Ability to select between a wide range of companies and private customers under their success definition is possible to provide a single proposal, according to the knowledge and skills of the coach.

- Large investments are not required, the sessions can be carried out at the home of the coach, at the clients not required, the sessions can be carried out knowledge.

- The combination of a thorough practical and theoretical preparation, persistence and sense of opportunity for exploring innovative ways on new poles of activity, result in a prosperous lifestyle and a substantial income.

Chapter 2 - Professional Projection

What should someone who wants to become a professional coach?

Reading this book is already a big step; add knowledge aspects of this interesting activity to visualize accurately the perspective offered, he must acquire consciousness of facets that are developed and resources that should have to become a professional coach.

Then he must select the area that excites him and feels that brings more value to people based on his own legitimate interests and the natural inclination of his talents.

Then he must choose the instance to qualify the type of coaching that he has chosen to examine the full agenda, and ensure that these degrees are guaranteed by certified bodies, preferably at international level, as the ICF (International Coach Federation), taught by teachers coaches.El fact that he is living the experience of being coaches provides a vision of being on both sides of the process. Through a classroom or remote mode, the choice depends on the availability of time and budget, as well as the alternative in which you feel more comfortable.

And practice. Practicing with everybody: family, friends, neighbors, acquaintances. Dare to say everyone you know what you do and asking for a chance to show it. In principle, not a serious exercise, but rather as an informal essay on which reassert learned items and draw his own dynamics coaching. Then it is feasible to offer talks to students and volunteer campaign.

The most important aspect to consider is that coaching, plus a productive activity, is a lifestyle, a commitment to creativity and excellence in all aspects of our daily activities. Its main tool is the ability to communicate; he must use it to promote his services, but above all its benefits, the positive impact of coaching in the lives of individuals and corporations is still something intangible in some environments and is a great area of opportunity to build new market niches.

Coaching process Benefits

The enormous effervescence that Coaching has acquired in recent times is because during the process can be acquired multiple benefits:

• Achieve what you want and do not have;

• Change what you have, but not useful;

• Make decisions that have been postponed;

• Encourage diversity of ideas;

• Fosters leave the comfort zone in a controlled manner to exploit new growth opportunities in all of life;

• Becomes an effective tool to solve everyday situations, such as one's fears, poor communication or lack of motivation.

• Make it a habit to focus on a target.

• During the sessions the coaches gains confidence in fields where previously dominated situations of distress;

• Achieve professional redesign; to extend the possibilities for action;

• Decisively help adaptability to change;

• Provides emotional resources to manage stress;

• Help learning to manage time;

• One of its main objectives is the pursuit of well-being;

• Break the limits of belief to go further;

• Leadership, conflict management, motivation of people, time management;

• Optimum performance is the result of the commitment of individuals and teams to perform the best that allow them their skills. This commitment is one of the consequences of the following conditions:

- It is understood he is doing and why it is important.

- Skills are acquired to perform the work and tasks expected of oneself.

- People feel appreciated for what they do and the difficulties of working become a personal challenge.

- You have the opportunity to improve when mistakes are made.

For the companies:

Coaching is important for companies because it is a process that facilitates adaptation to changes in an efficient and effective way because:

• Renews and mobilizes the commitments directing human core values;

• It stimulates and directs people towards achieving unprecedented results;

• Renews relationships and increases the effectiveness of communication in human systems;

• Predisposes members for collaboration, teamwork and consensus building, and

• Projects the potential of people, enabling them to achieve goals that otherwise are considered unreachable.

Where and how the coach gets to his customers?

Customers for Coaching services are as diverse as each professional dedicated to it. The best customer is the one who can be provided the best service by the Coach, that is whom the coach skills and distinctive style will bring the greatest benefit. At first, it is one of the most absorbing activities of professional projection since factors such as the area of specialization, geographical position, demand and the entrenchment of the culture of coaching at each site are variants determined by the circumstances in each case. However, there are general guidelines of reference on which it is possible to achieve tangible results in terms of time quite acceptable, although, as always, depends on the commitment, boldness and creativity with the coach invest in this task.

Clarity of actions

- A coach should know so well describe what it does and how it benefits with it that can explain it in 15 seconds. When he does he has found the greatest benefit that can provide, and that is the best argument for a customer decision, then he can complement preparing a speech for 30 seconds and then may extend by one, two five. In this way, the coach establishes a priority panorama of their sales, which are the key to his promotional strategy.

Once established activity and benefits, The Coach seeks whom will benefit by his accumulation of challenges and life experiences, achievements and professional scopes, fields that he knows he comprises and is competent; all the compendium of knowledge that he has cultivated: values, beliefs, interests, intuitions that make up a vision and skills that enhance his performance as coach. An important clue that can help him is through examining himself: the best he has obtained from its own process of coaching, and through that trigger, could help solve the problems of someone else.

Knowing his target.

Who is the sort of person whom he could help more effectively to solve their problems? What is their habit? Are young or old? Men or women? What interests motivate them? Why would they seek his services? This criterion is based not only on the particular needs and problems that have as individuals or companies but also in their goals and desires. Coaching has much to do with them.

Where does he must find his first clients? A good start is to develop a database of his acquaintances, friends, and coworkers to whom he can offer these services; then he can expand in other social and professional fields and finally to the specific spheres that would like to explore.

Making contact is very important, but he needs to remember, especially when we talk about companies or well-known characters, the coach already knows who they are, but they do not know to him, so that should get their attention, arouse their interest, to incite their desire, encourage their commitment. He must set the environment, structuring the message clear and interesting way.

In principle, it is very useful to observe his colleagues, how they promote their services and why they do so, in this way it is possible to find or design an appropriate strategy. Resources are basically:

E-mail

The cheapest, but one of the less effective if it is not addressed to the right person. In the case of businesses is indispensable contact who makes hiring decisions, seeking to establish empathy through a personalized, colorful, agile and concise mail, thinking what would attract attention, and how much time he would devote to read that email if he were that person.

Brochures

The massive nature of brochures allows to deliver them to passersby on an avenue busy in a place that brings together prospective customers; can also be hand out in events like business conventions or lectures or trade shows on specific sectors.

Advertisements

From a classified ad in a local newspaper to a flat in specialized magazines on industries or productive sectors; there are free and paid advertising inserts that ensure more readers, and therefore more likely to be hired.

Lectures and seminars

There are different events that can be profitable to know potential clients, from conferences, trade fairs and expos, lectures and conferences related to the productive sector that coach decides to explore. If he has the ability as a speaker, could offer free talks.

Websites

With the mastery of basic technology and digital marketing, any person can create functional pages, affordable for all budgets that can include free templates. As in all of these options, he does not need to be an expert but must acquire the knowledge of where to get the resources he requires.

Blogs

This new genre of writing is based on creating interesting content on a personal concept to generate traffic on a website, with a component of marketing to spread the name of who produces it and the benefits it offers, can have its own blog or write as a guest on a colleague already known and written material required to have an updated information; a great plus is this tool is practically free.

Online forums

It is a more direct contact that has many potential advantages, because there is an interactive communication first hand, which allows meeting participants and how they function in that environment, is a great way to meet their needs, demands and type of services they require. Once the coach can establish a link with the forum participants must follow them, sending them messages regularly, greeting them and inquiring about their activities and informing them about services and promotions he offers, as well as data relevant to those prospects with, in order to build a bond of trust, meet their needs to make an offer about something that really valued, and above all, be the first alternative when they require services that coach offers.

This is an environment where competition is like any other, but there are many unexplored areas waiting for a coach. The task is to find and test some approaches without the expectation of getting clients immediately: it is a first approximation, he is still exploring the market, although probably he might be surprised if the first opportunity arises; the coach must be prepared for everything.

Promotion and dissemination

Schools, universities, business organizations, associations, are excellent venues for bring together people who share an interest in learning and improve their knowledge and skills; all bodies and institutions often have an Internet site where they talk about their visions, missions, ie their business or institutional philosophy, so that using the Internet is a powerful tool because it allows access to such information.

Promotion and diffusion

Schools, universities, business organizations, associations, are excellent venues for bring together people who share an interest in learning and improve their knowledge and skills; all bodies and institutions often have an Internet site where they talk about their visions, missions, i.e. their business or institutional philosophy, so that using the Internet is an excellent tool because it allows access to such information.

Networking

It is essential to deepen the knowledge of marketing and sales that may have: no business that dispenses with these activities.

Chapter 3 - The Dynamics of Coaching

What actually happens when a coach works with someone?

In fact, during a session the task of the coach is to formulate specific questions for the coaches systematically finds answers that lead to a comprehensive view of his situation, identifying limitations, which are his own beliefs, attitudes, and emotions, so he confronts the validity of his pre-established concepts and let him externalize their thoughts, aspirations and more legitimate concerns on which to set a target and organizing a scheme of action. The meaning of the questions varies at each stage. Leading questions allow to delve into the deeper levels of problems and interrelate the aspects that will produce more conflict, and builds a diagram of his pattern of behavior. Inferential questions allow accessing logic solutions, outlining a scheme of possible actions on which to develop an action plan. Having established the context follows the stage of engagement with the first actions to achieve, making room for experimentation and even calculated risk. In subsequent sessions are given to monitoring and evaluating the actions taken and the process of the first session is repeated if necessary.

What sort's specializations we can find in the Coaching?

Coaching has proven successful in different fields, so, range of action is very broad, there are even coaches for love, however, its main activity is developed in these areas:

• Personal development: Identify the objectives to project his skills in different areas: projection skills, academic goals, leadership skills, decision making, negotiation skills and conflict resolution, integrating them into coherent actions to achieve them;

• Business: focused on the overall improvement of a company or sections of it, aspects such as the creation of leaders in organizational structure, internal communications, team building, logistics, and marketing among others,usually aimed at senior officers;

• Executive: Developing an individual's professional activity, team organization, pressure management, crisis management, and acquisition of specific skills of their field, self-promotion, motivation, business relationships, projection performance and career plans.

• Welfare: as a life coach, aimed at improving the quality of health,the decision to change harmful habits, spiritual peace, emotional stability, family, friends, family, leisure time.

Coaching styles

There is three major school of coaching, although arising from different fundamentals, contribute and take concepts to each other, contextualizing their own essential guidelines.

American School

Founded by Thomas Leonard, is the most executive and aspirational of the three major schools; increases self-esteem and challenges its participants to turn to action by projecting the best of themselves, reflecting the American characteristic vision of success. His proposals gravitate about a model called 5 x 15 which are five related elements each with five races, 15 sorters, 15 products and 15 frames. Which are set forth below in condensed form:

Five interrelated elements:

1. 15 Coaching Skills: basic skills that should develop the Coach to establish a successful session;

2. 15 Clarifiers: reveal the essence of what tries to express the client, guiding the session to what is most important;

3. 15 Products: contributions that the coach can offer your client from this collaboration;

4. 15 Marks: concepts proposed by the coach to fracture the mental maps in potential of coaches by others broader, and;

5. 15 Style points: resources that the coach to establish a profitable relationship with your customer with your client.

Critics of this system considered this devoid of conceptual background and transformational effectiveness.

European School

Its founder was Timothy Gallwey, of American origin. This school, rather than the delirious longing for American success, opts for understanding, awareness and building self-confidence on the concept of inner game which set that the action of all human effort requires two intervention flows interacting: the outside game, challenging circumstances and environmental obstacles to achieve tangible goals, and the inside game, whose stage is the mind, in which the elements to face are the lack of sustained attention, limiting beliefs, the recurring question, self-criticism, and especially the fear, whose interference impedes the flow of our performance potential; This stream flows freely to the extent we increase our potential and decreased interference, and is achieved with a state of mind calm and focused. Timothy Gallwey himself summarizes this philosophy in a sentence. "How you play this game usually makes the difference between success and failure"

Developing your system puts over his book "The Inner Game of Tennis" in which he outlined six key principles.

1.   The keyword is to leave: one must bet on trust rather on the effort. If the body already knows how to perform an action you have to let it happen. If it does not yet know, then you have to let it learn;

2. Leave the judgment to him. Interrupting the flow of performance for questioning about whether you are doing right or wrong, it leads to excess thoughts,

doubt and lack of concentration. Negative and positive judgments are equally harmful, but ignore the judgments does not mean to overlook mistakes: it is to be aware of the actual magnitude of the situation, without adding anything;

3. Learn to trust. Inside the inner game it performs a frustrating dialogue between the doubts and possibilities that are perceived from outside information, it is because a part of itself does not trust his abilities if it develops otherwise, this dialogue would not exist.

4. Respect the natural process of learning. This process occurs in all people, without making great efforts, if given the opportunity. In childhood there is not a judgment about what is being done right or wrong, it is not at stake self-esteem nor doubt the ability himself, each error is part of the learning process;

5. The Art of relaxed concentration. It is the most important concept in the inner game. It is based on thinking we can do our job without trying too hard. A

combined feeling between relaxation, excitement, and abstraction, and

6. Create an image of the desired result. In times of stress is difficult to maintain calm the mind, the power of an image inside game is more than the display of achievement, is to project calm and attention in each movement.

Chilean school

Also called Ontological Coaching, builds on the ideas of the minister and philosopher Chilean Fernando Flores, who along with Julio Olalla and Rafael Echeverria has guided these principles to business leadership, being Echeverria its main diffuser and who coined the name the system, "Ontological language" through his book of the same name. This school focuses on providing transformational processes from an ontological correspondence, composed of body, emotion, and language. It is based on three postulates and two principles:

Postulates

1. We interpret human beings as linguistic beings. Language is what makes humans what they are, and its phenomena are understood from this point of view.

2. The language is generative, reality is not only described by it, also is created. We exist because of language, by it; we shape the reality and the environment.

3. Human beings are created themselves in the language and through it, this means our ability to reinvent ourselves, taking an active role in our evolution, what we want to become.

Two principles

1. We do not know how things are, only how we see and perceive.

The brain interprets what the senses perceive and live in worlds interpretation. We are all observers from a different reality, or rather, a different angle of reality, so no one is certain that things are how we perceive it.

There is no path to absolute truth, only we can see ours, this compendium of knowledge discovers both what is seen as one who observes and how. This is the principle that we are worth to understand the interpretive world of our client. It reveals who is from what we see and how we interpret them. These are expressed in language which never is neutral, they provide us interpretations that add or wrest power to the possibilities of life.

2. Action generates being.

The transformational power rotates in two directions, what we determine what we do, but also our actions allow transform us, shaping our identity; If you learn to observe differently, you learn to act differently.

Coercive Coaching

Although not called themselves by that term, because it would be self-accusatory, it is easy to recognize by its organizational structure based on multilevel marketing and invasive activities of privacy, in fact, neither intended, nor methods can be considered coaching because it is not based on precursor questions for auto-generative answers, and objectives are determined by the instructor; It handled through seminars in different phases, based on inducing levels of fear or anxiety as a control method in attitude in those involved in these dynamics, confronting them with their not overcome emotional conflicts and causing disturbing experiences and altered states of consciousness, low the argument that it is a preparation for life and in order to leave the comfort zone and get over fears, confronting them. It is recommended to be careful with this type of training, because has been questioned about the lack of preparation of their trainers, also its ethical, economic and manipulation of groups principles, which assume the docility of the participant to the orders of his instructors as reflection their level of commitment, personal boundaries are diluted and the notion of individuality is lost.

What skills should have a Coach?

The coach is a kind of sounding board and his cache's alter ego, a type of external consciousness that makes the questions he dares not ask.

• Interpersonal communication: He is the axis along which evolves Coaching work in all its aspects, the effectiveness of the process depends on the ability of the coach to establish links with his client at different levels.

• The ability to ask the right questions in particular contexts. A well-structured sequence of questions in the search for answers that can arise from anywhere.

• Able to continuously sustain a thoughtful and attentive listening.

• A deep commitment to service. Any activity focused on service should be aimed at the customer's benefit, such as coaching, impact over important aspects of the welfare of the coaches and focused dedication to his satisfaction is fundamental.

• Analytical skills: Being receptive to information captured to discern the meaning of a concept, to design the questions that fragment the answers into lines for simpler reasoning.

• Assertiveness: a difficult skill, it requires emotional balance and a very strong attachment to those adopted values to expressing disagree without fear or exalted emotions.

Chapter 4 - What Are Principles that Must Have a Coach?

The principles are based on three aspects.

Ethics: When working with intimate emotions of the client has access to their most vulnerable areas. Any action by the Coach for personal gain or to cause harm, is a betrayal of customer confidence, being sometimes very subtle this line of integrity must remain attentive to not pass it involuntarily. Also, there are problems when the customer exceeds the scope of competence of Coach, this must recognize the fact, and remit his client to the specialist in the field: advisor, psychologist, trainer, therapist or consultant, as appropriate.

Confidentiality: All information on the coaches extracted at any stage of the process must be protected indisputably, except with the knowledge of serious crimes, depending on the regulations of each country, outside this exception, any leakage of information is unethical and illegal, also will affect the atmosphere of trust that must prevail in the relationship with the coaches.

Confidence: While the above two points have to do with this aspect, confidence in this context refers not only to a determining factor, is also a feeling that the customer must perceive to consolidate the flow of communication with him.

Clarity: The communication must be direct and specific, without allowing gaps of uncertainty or misinterpretation.

Support: It means providing the resources required by the coaches in this process, knowledge, materials, emotional support, and guidance.

Mutuality: The full vision and common objectives in terms of importance and phases in time and actions to achieve a goal shared by all team members' integration.

Perspective: To adopt the point of view of subordinates through questions involving the coach with them, revealing the reality of the team members. It is useless to guess what they think and feel, it is always necessary to ask.

Taking risks: Our culture punishes more error than apathy, feeds the paradox of requiring the initiative, but without accepting the risks involved. Is essential to enable team members to actuate resolutely with confidence that errors will not be punished with dismissal, and their competence is not questioned, provided that this setback becomes an element of learning and improvement.

What is the difference between a good and a bad coach?

• Respects rhythms, times and needs of his clients, but also encourages them to leave your comfort zone and unproductive emotional states;

• The balance in the emotional rapport is a key factor, being immersed in the client's problem is important to establish empathy necessary to understand the logic of their emotions and behavior, but there must be an emotional distance so as not to be influenced by his emotional energy and lose the ability to analyze the whole picture objectively. The reverse is also harmful, the too pragmatic analysis ends up being a laboratory study in which key emotional aspects are lost in the advancement of the coaching process. Obviously, the worst is the coach devoid of any interest in the problems of the coaches, thinking that only the approach to the questions of a static model is sufficient to achieve the process. Many Coaches do it consciously or unconsciously, due to a lack of empathy with your client or because some aspect of the problem of coaches which resonates in their own conflicts, and

• The preparation for the sessions. Once the Coach determines its field of expertise he finds that customers profile is similar, so the format of the questions are usually similar from one session to another, leading to custom and forget that each client presents a circumstance different and may lose sensitivity to the direction of the important questions.

•Upgrade. Any change in social dynamics side cause effects in the lives of people, not being aware of the scope of these variables means a risk of our coaching model is becoming obsolete. In such a dynamic environment, Coach should keep in mind that the while more varied is his clientele, will be more diverse fields on that he will have to be updated, and the customer, very frequently, presents new conflicts that before were not raised.

• A good coach is itself an example of openness to new interpretations, overcoming the fear of what is unknown. It is an explorer of possibilities.

• A good Coach opens questions to possibilities arising from the free flow of thought of his client, attentive to the answers he seeks and focuses attention again if the focus on the theme is lost.

• The approach of the questions, a good coach anticipates its effect to an aspect he wants to know. The tone, intent, specificity, and the timing are as important as your ability to interpret the answers, to elucidate their meaning with no margin for error.

• A good Coach creates a climate of discovery. Suspends premature judgment and listens to find connections between ideas.

• In the case of group sessions, he recognizes and encourages the contributions they can provide. Also articulates the shared understanding. Collects and shares collective discoveries, for it, eliminates the boundaries of function, hierarchy, discipline, or occupation.

Chapter 5 - Questions

Why ask?

Asking questions is the essence of coaching, unlike other development techniques in which knowledge of counselor, teacher or mentor are transferred, the aim is that from process analysis and search, arising conclusions are generated by the same coachee, the primary task of the coach is to create the right atmosphere and manages through a series of key questions, the order of ideas that lead to these conclusions to establish them a consistent manner.

Through a suitable approach to new dimensions of reflection, questions are discovered, a critical approach from different perspectives facilitating the process of self-discovery.

How to be efficient in developing questions

The questions are the fundamental component of the dynamics; they cause the unlocking of the confusing concepts. Each should consider taking into account a target. Keep in mind that the answer to a question can provide several answers, there is much on what is said, how it is said and what silent express. Coach acts then as a benevolent detective who reviews other deeper answers which are not the same that client knows, and this is one of the most exciting aspects of coaching: the coaches discovers the solution to the most hidden enigmas in his inside, this is liberating and transcendental.

In Coaching, each question follows a strategy. Knowing the type of questions allows us to know and use the huge arsenal of resources as Coach have available.

The starting point for effective questioning is active listening. Agatha Christy said that if you let someone speak enough you can end up discovering the truth; there is indeed something of police interrogation, especially when the goal is to get the coaches leaves his comfort zone to confront his reality or his fears.

Usually, it starts with open questions, which allow the answer extends to expose an overview according is taking shape the direction the conversation. Closed questions seeking very specific answers, which also prevent that the coaches circumvents, or loses focus point.

The short questions that give space to specific answers are the most effective in the coaches, they do not allow him to digress and indicate a concrete sense to the answer

- "Divide and conquer" is a mathematical algorithm very applicable in this context as a resource of maieutics.

If the issue is very complex to explain, it is divided into simpler fragments until the solution of the parties becomes obvious. The answer of the main problem is built with the intermediate solutions found.

Types of questions

The literal comprehension: knowing, understanding, measuring the ability to learn, recognize explicit information, which is the main difference between the analysis and the interference. The analysis interprets, synthesizes, and distinguishes the main ideas from secondary:

Interference, meanwhile supposed concludes, makes a judgment. It is to derive implicit information from explicit data.

From the process in question is referred to the following categories of pergolas:

• Questions icebreaker;

• Control questions;

• Questions filter;

• Thematic or substantive;

• Standardization: Open, closed, semi-open;

• Direct and indirect questions,

• Inductive and deductive;

• Appreciative Questions: What is not working and how to fix it? What is working and how to promote it? What is possible here and who cares? What is the problem here and what cause it?

• Questions to focus collective attention on their situation. What is important to you and why do you care? What brought us to this research? What is our purpose here? What is the deeper purpose (The great because) this is truly worthy of our best effort? What opportunities can see in our specific situation? What we know so far and we still need to learn about it? What are problems and opportunities in this situation? What are assumptions that we need to test the situation here? What we are not seeing, or we need seeing more clearly? What has been the greatest learning, knowledge or discovery so far?

• Questions that create breakthrough what would it take to create change on this issue? What could happen that would allow us to feel engaged and empowered? ¿What requires our immediate attention going forward? If our success was guaranteed. What bold steps could choose? How can we support each other to affect the next steps? What unique contribution can offer each of us? What problems might we face and how we can address them? What could we do today to make the difference in the future? What is the next level of thinking we should achieve?

On Coaching, the most important question is one that gets an answer which generates more key questions in the spirit of the coaches. A behavior pattern shift occurs when a question is performed from the inside of a current paradigm, which can be answered when paradigm breaks.

A powerful question generates curiosity in the listener, stimulates reflective conversation, brings to the surface underlying problems, and invites creativity and new possibilities. It generates power and advancement by means of original attention channels. Evokes more questions. Touches a deeper meaning. It arises in such a way that induces new approaches from answers that we think knowing.

Pyramid technique:

In a specific application, determines the priority of words, from the more to the less powerful for your specific resolution.

What? Who? How? When? Where? Why?

Architecture questions. Criteria to establish a question are:

• Is this question relevant to the treated subject?

• Is this a question that can really give you an answer known?

• What do I want to get doing this question? That is, what kind of conversation, meanings, and feelings that evoke imagination in the coachee?

• Is it likely that new ideas could incite questions and answers?

• What assumptions or beliefs are rooted in the way the question is built?

• Is this question could generate hope, imagination, commitment, creative effort or is likely to increase the focus on problems and obstacles in the past?

• Is this a kind of question that leaves room for further consultations that may be exploited in the future?

The strongest questions involving hopes and ideals of the people values; always must keep in mind that the way you ask determines the response. It is very common in everyday life, we make thoughtless questions delegating to our interlocutor the responsibility to interpret the sense of what we said: one of the great problems of communication. One should not underestimate this element. The act of asking is not so easy.

Instant response questions do not necessarily reflect the values of the person, but if more immediate concerns.

A series of questions are also generated to be used to close a concept and questions are posting in different ways.

Unless a question "Why?" can be carefully crafted, it is easy to incite a defensive response. An indirect way of ask could be better: "I wonder why that would have happened this to you"

With questions, power is obtained or granted, none is bad because it can be part of a strategy; you just have to be aware of each step.

Common mistakes and how to correct

Working for a client who is outside the profile of Coach: A customer who does not like to him, or that is handled in a different cultural context, or the circumstances of the client are beyond his expertise, approaches or interest, the coaches could not appreciate values and benefits that coach offers, and if he do not have the ability to motivate, will become a frustrating experience for both. Another important mistake is Not knowing detect whether the client needs a Coaching, therapy, a mentor or just a break, only fits this type of errors.

In other cases, customers are not ready for a coaching process. He has to be direct, but diplomatic in explaining the reasons; in fact, it is advisable to settle this possibility before starting the process and having colleagues to whom can direct that client.

Involve his conclusions on the customer. For good intention or see from his perspective what the customer does not see, either because it is what the customer expects from him among the confusion or simply to break a silence, he can fall into the trap of interference of own judgments. Of course, the coach must generate his own reflections, but should only serve as exploratory shafts. If at any time contributes with some opinions, should be to open another line of possibilities.

Avoid advising:

- Not give instructions on what to do or how to act;

- Not judge;

- Not press;

- Be very rigid in the system.

- Paternalistic attitudes: As introductory element to the first session should disclose clearly the client the role played by the coach in this process, he is an active partner in their life project, therefore, he should not assume the treatment like parent, guardian or unquestioned authority and not allow emotions to wake up during the sessions affect the objectivity of coach.

- Not be able to adopt the communicational style of his client. Each person has formed its own pattern of communication; some are very specific, while others need to digress a bit before landing his thoughts, this depends not only on the personality but also of the circumstance. It considers often that for coaches the tension generated by a session is compared to a job interview. The Coach must realize this communication style and adapt his own dynamics to set factors of identification.

To assume that the customer is sincere to expose their fears. There is a strong natural and educational resistance to share fears, to the point that people do not quite admit directly nor to themselves, which is understandable because it is the implicit proof of their vulnerability, but this is the same reason that they are so difficult to solve, because to overcome a fear, it is necessary to expose in his bare essence for submission to its objective scrutiny. The strategy is to pose the same question under different approaches to compare the consistency of responses and raise customer awareness that half of the solution for his challenges is focused on confronting those fears.

- Press coaches to get all his goals from the first session.

-Allow the Conditional. "I would have to" "I should," "I would like" are words that do not lead to action. Questions should be short. How? Where? For what? When?

- Be impatient or to lose respect for the client.

- Create confusion or stress for free in the coaches.

- Ask questions out of context without reasonable justification. These questions occur more often than is believed; an inherent feature of good Coach is curiosity, and as a customer easily lost the direction of the target, led by a free association of ideas, the Coach can be carried away by their own associations, interest in secondary aspects of the conversation or by to some unconscious curiosity. Each question is a trigger in his attention, and the coachee is going to try to find a consistent message, if he does not find it, he will be confused, and if that is not the intention of Coach this will play against him.

- Standardize how to act with all customers. There exploration questions that serve to glimpse the perspective of the coaches. Given the same circumstances each client, develops its own perception according to their temperament and interpretation, according to their own experiences, the key is to place importance on their priorities and at this point shaping strategic questions.

-The Arrogance: A Coach is a service provider, not someone who is over others. He is a professional with effective remedies that assisting competent people to achieve their goals; no more, no less.

Chapter 6 - Coaching Process

Conversational models, research goal setting parameters and instructions step by step

Coaching is based on three fundamental principles are called the Three Pillars of Coaching and we must be aware that the development of the talks should be aimed in the direction of the same.

1- Taking consciousness;

2- Auto belief, and

2- Responsibility.

There are multiple variables of a coaching session and considering the procedures of the various schools and objectives, but the GROW model reflects the overall structure in terms of methods and purpose of all the others, so it serves as a general reference to other conversational Coaching models.

GROW model

Used with equal success to achieving objectives or as a remedial tool, so named because it is an anagram of the phases that composes it.

G- Goal: What do I want? This question gives direction to the efforts, all the longings, what I really need and want to happen and what I'd just like to happen? What would happen in my life if I caught what I want to achieve? Measurable and achievable goals that settle a precedent of success on which trust is built to achieve greater challenges are set.

R- Reality: Where am I? At this stage we locate our current reality, where do I am exactly at this time? What is the reason? What would happen if I do not change? What are the consequences? This is the time to expound, with total freedom, the more intimate thoughts, free of judgment on what should be or meet the expectations that others expect, emotional limitations, beliefs or attitudes are identified.

O Options: What I can do? Freed from these constraints they are creatively displayed variants of action, and resources are sought, alternatives and evaluated the benefits and costs that are willing to assume. This is the process of reinvention and renewal, and the Coach must be very careful that the propositive questions do not become options that customer must interpret as measures he has to assume.

W- Will: Commitment, What will I do? This step requires a great conviction. The selected plan has to be taken realistically considered as the steps to achieve the proposed goal. What will I do? How do I do it? When? Where? How do I get support? What resources should I procure? What obstacles must be overcome? What chance I have to get it?

In the midst of this process intermediate stages happen which are discussed below.

Stages of a session

The conversational models vary according to the objectives to achieve and develop according to their context of shared trials and before the conversation events, however, there are key elements that must be reiterated that serve as a common reference to the coaching to be the basis of their purpose, but which fits within a broad universe of variables.

It should be considered that although the coaching as a development tool as well as the remedial measure is used, it should not treat anything as a problem, but as projects to achieve, this neutralizes any negative connotation on the session and the issue to be addressed.

Before starting the first session, it must be established with the client several aspects which he has to understand to operate better along with it. This is the stage of knowledge.

Coach ensures the process, not the result, which depends on openness, interest, commitment and honesty of the coaches in his responses.

Features of the session

- The practice of values, for example, respect, commitment, permit, to name a few;

- The relationship between the two partners is a personal project;

- Suggest the possibility that a good chemistry between them could not be set, and determine what to do about it;

- Probably the client does not have previous experience in this type of dynamics, and usually expect it to be the coach who takes all the initiative, he should encourage them to take an active part from the start;

- Coaches expectations are clarified: "What do you expect this?"

 - His willingness to change is evaluated: "What are you willing?"

RAPPORT

- Client mood is recorded and focuses if it is necessary, ie, he is tranquilized and induces him to recognize the emotional state in which it is located. In this state it is essential the customer can express with complete freedom, and give tacit permission about conflicting aspects. Coach set an atmosphere of trust and emotional opening.

This process is the pacing, and in him, through it all resources are put in place to achieve that may affect the emotionality of the coaches, as a relaxed and intimate space, using a tone and rhythm of safe and soothing voice, along with elements of nonverbal communication, often more expressive than words, as the intention of the gaze, body posture and breathing rate. The set of arguments and actions that induce a state of confidence and enthusiasm "What would he need to hear to trust me?", "How I could take him out of his comfort zone without being invasive or lose his confidence ? ".

This is determined by a number of criteria which almost all respond in a universal way but also involved their own temperament factors that we have to consider on what his attitude and style of conversation may reveal to us; because a rapport is different for each client.

The basic process of Coaching starts from identifying goals, specifying objectives, strengths, and weaknesses. But it happens in cases where the coaches is very confused to establish its priority, so it is sometimes preferable to reverse the order for the second step, analyze your current situation. At this time the customer exposes the outlook of his circumstances as he interprets them based on their personality, beliefs, assumed limits and previous experiences.

Context: It is the reference line on which the coach and the client will collaborate, this the stage where awareness begins with the approach of the situation to deal with. That Breaking Point arises when there is a problem to solve or an achievement to get. Sometimes, if it comes to business coaching, the company decides what the topic to work is. If the coachee attended privately, it may during the session he realizes that was not the look I wanted to work on principle and this point is changed to be treated.

During this first phase of questions, the coach must be attentive, not only in responses, should also observe the body language and reactions of the coachee when responding.

By setting the target to be solved, questions aimed at determining the importance and context of this particular issue and their interrelationships within the spectrum of customer concerns, the current situation is evaluated, but even more, sets out how the client gives shape and structure to his problems, how faces them. At this point, the open questions give way to comprehensive customer´s view and encourage talk.

Here are some questions that correspond to this stage;

"What would you like to solve this coaching session?"

"Why do you want to address this point?"

"Why do not you have decided to resolve it before?

"In the order of your personal and professional priorities which number from 1 to 10 has this?"

"How do you feel about this challenge?"

"If I were a six-year-old child how you explain it to me?"

"If I were the alter ego of your problem, what would you say to me?"

"How would improve accomplish this in other facets of your life?"

"What if you do not decide to solve it?"

"What prevents you overcome it?" Virtually all reasons are due to adverse circumstances, lack of resources (materials, skills, and abilities), lack of motivation and fears.

"What would be the worst case scenario?"

"Do you think this obstacle is itself a cause or the result of another aspect of background?"

Inquiry

Through systematic questions is guided to the coaches to know it and to create a scenario of how you would feel taking other attitudes and actions in specific situations, accessing a universe of options which, from his old pattern of beliefs had not considered. A resource is to repeat in other words what the client has said, validating the interpretation of his concepts and to confront the validity of these arguments and assumptions, identifying whether they are real obstacles or assumptions, whose validity exists only in his compendium of beliefs, i.e., facts or interpretations.

Sometimes the answer received responds to several questions or triggers new questions, if there are still any aspects of those he wants to deepen, the coach has to pose them more specifically.

Commitment

Finding solutions: This is the phase where he finds vicious circles and the major frustrations are stuck because efforts do not result in solution; more than the problem, the feeling of anxiety results of not considered able to solve it, so it is necessary to focus again the coaches, if he has lost calm, as well as exploring the universe of possibilities, acquiring awareness that there are affordable solutions increases the anemic level of client. At this point the coaches already has a realistic picture of their circumstances over which organizes a reasonable and pragmatic plan of action, he is aware of its real resources and obstacles to overcome; the course of the questions already are not focused in the "what" but about the "How" Devising and evaluating the different options available at this stage, delineating a scenario of all possible actions through different views on selected alternative, to shape an articulated plan

The questions focus on finding innovative solutions ,.In This step is advisable to apply creativity techniques Eduard de Bono to design these questions aimed at the intellectual action.

"What did you do before this?"

"To what extent these actions have served you?"

"What have you learned from them?"

"What do you think would need to happen for this goal be reached?"

"What would be the best outcome?"

"Which of your skills and strengths you think would be useful in this project?"

"If you had a box of talents they serve to achieve what you want, what would be the three to choose?"

"Who could help you in this purpose and how?"

"What of your personality aspects have to relax or allow to flow to advance in this area?"

"How would you do differently?"

"If the conditions were ideal, what are three ways you could succeed at this point?"

"In the current scenario which one would you choose?"

"If an answer could solve the whole thing, what would be the question?"

"How would solve a person you trust this?"

"What would be the actions to take if this plan does not advance?"

"What conclusions get all this?"

"What would be the first action to take?"

Responsibility: It is the stage of genuine commitment to the selected solution, in which the coaches implements the first steps immediately, which will be followed by subsequent coaching sessions.

If the above processes were well developed, the coaches is ready for this moment, otherwise, you will have to rethink the purpose of the session.

"Why are you willing to take on this challenge?"

"What aspects of you should reorient?"

"When will you start to work on the first goals?" (In this subsection it does not refer to results, but actions to achieve them)

"How to evaluate the steps?"

"What results would you want to achieve before next session?"

To expose all process a condensed form: it is reveal, communicate, specify, and create.

Once you have selected a solution, the primary actions are set to carry out and timelines to achieve them.

Agreement.

Because coaching is a service should be laid down in writing the relevant aspects of the agreement establishing the Coach and coaches, taking care that this document is specific.

A single topic.

Aspects to be set are as follows

- Objectives of contract;

- Objective of process -objective of meeting;

- Validation of the contract by the coaches;

- Openness to new interpretations and possibilities.

- Agree on action plan;

- Closing;

- Tracing;

- New possibilities;

- Recognition of coaches commitment, and

- Application to other domains.

Conclusion

Coaching Innovates and renews. That is the spirit that creates and that is its raison d'etre. In the field of evolution and excellence does not exclude anything. The Coach is an explorer of possibilities, in fact, experimentation is part of their job, with many fields of application, and research tools are resources that should be used for many reasons.

You must understand the social dynamics that influence on a person whom you provide your services, advances in other alternative areas that provide useful elements in their work, commercial and technological environment of the companies which hire to you, the knowledge that manages to further their skills. It is a relatively new discipline that responds to needs to the social dynamics that impact diverse areas of life at all levels. The Coach should move forward with these changes.

 The following paragraphs are references to start to develop research methods aimed at their own development guidelines are set forth below.

Related Concepts

• Law of Attraction.

• Creativity, Eduard de Bono.

• Emotional Intelligence, Daniel Goleman

• Mental Science and new thinking. William Walker Atkinson, Neville Goddard

• Logotherapy, Viktor Frankl.

• Organizational psychology. The works on the psychological processes of each individual inherent in an organization.

• Social Psychology. Studies the influence of groups in each person.

• The related fields that are based coaching philosophy, psychology, NLP, ontological language,

• The Mayéutica is the oldest reference related to discovering the truth from questions. Credited to Socrates, he helped give birth to ideas, his phrase "I know that I know nothing" takes context to assume that it is an ignorant and its function is not to be the one who finds the truth, but only raise the petunias to be his interlocutor who finds. The art of light spirits. It basically consists of a question and confronts each answer with a new question to filter a true response that integrates the partial truth of the above.

• Educational Psychology: It studies the processes of personal and collective education of human beings.

• Developmental Psychology: Consider all stages of life, from conception to death, analyzing their behavioral, physical, cognitive, social and emotional changes.

• Experimental Psychology: It is aimed at observation, investigation and registration of new methods of study

• Personality Psychology: It analyzes the mental processes that govern the conduct and behavior.

• Behaviorism: Study how the environment shapes and influence behavior.

• Humanism: The behavior is governed by self-image, that subjective perception and the desire for personal growth is built.

• Cognitivism: Human behavior from the perspective of the mental process of information.

• Gestalt: The whole is greater than the sum of the parts. Shares many principles of coaching as awareness, the "Realize" The importance of focusing on the here and now. Breaks the barriers of perception and assumes that the origin of all psychological disorders lies in our inability to effectively integrate the facets that make up our personality into a harmonious whole. Healthy individuals organize their expectations of experience around well-defined needs that frame your system behavior.

http://documents.mx/documents/whitmore-john-coaching-pdf.html

https://wordpresstestblog2.files.wordpress.com/2013/09/25-free-coaching-tools-and-techniques.pdf

http://www.forbes.com/2010/04/28/coaching-talent-development-leadership-managing-ccl.html

http://www.aitsl.edu.au/docs/default-source/professional-growth-resources/performance-and-development-resources/3-what-techniques-do-coaches-use-final-20140124.pdf

http://lateralaction.com/articles/creative-coaching/

http://www.theworldcafe.com/wp-content/uploads/2015/07/art_of_powerful_questions.pdf

Notes

Lightning Source UK Ltd.
Milton Keynes UK
UKOW05f2043020517
300357UK00010B/1277/P